AMAZING SNAKES!

RAINBOW BOAS

BY CHRIS BOWMAN

EPIC

BELLWETHER MEDIA • MINNEAPOLIS, MN

EPIC BOOKS are no ordinary books. They burst with intense action, high-speed heroics, and shadows of the unknown. Are you ready for an Epic adventure?

This edition first published in 2014 by Bellwether Media, Inc.

Library of Congress Cataloging-in-Publication Data

Bowman, Chris, 1990- author.
Rainbow Boas / by Chris Bowman.
pages cm. – (Epic. Amazing Snakes!)
Summary: "Engaging images accompany information about rainbow boas. The combination of high-interest subject matter and light text is intended for students in grades 2 through 7"– Provided by publisher.
Audience: Ages 7-12.
Audience: Grades 2 to 7.
Includes bibliographical references and index.
ISBN 978-1-62617-125-1 (hardcover : alk. paper)
1. Rainbow boa–Juvenile literature. I. Title.
QL666.O63B68 2014
597.96'7–dc23

2013050081

TABLE OF CONTENTS

WHAT ARE RAINBOW BOAS?

Rainbow boas are beautiful snakes with multicolored skin. They grow up to 7 feet (2.1 meters) long.

No Leg to Stand On

Rainbow boas have tiny back legs. They are too small for the boas to use.

WHERE RAINBOW BOAS LIVE

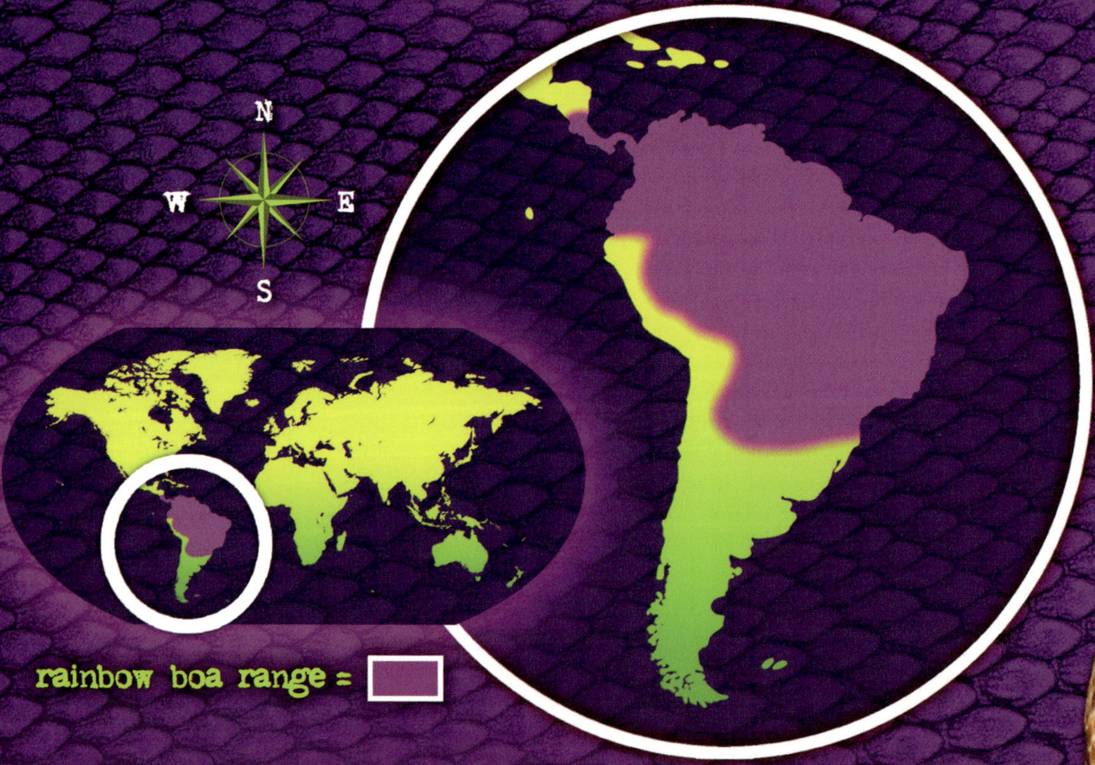

Rainbow boas are found in Central and South America. They live in forests, **rain forests**, and **savannahs**. Their **scutes** help them slither across the ground and on low branches.

Water Shy

Rainbow boas are excellent swimmers. However, they usually stay away from water.

SHINING SKIN

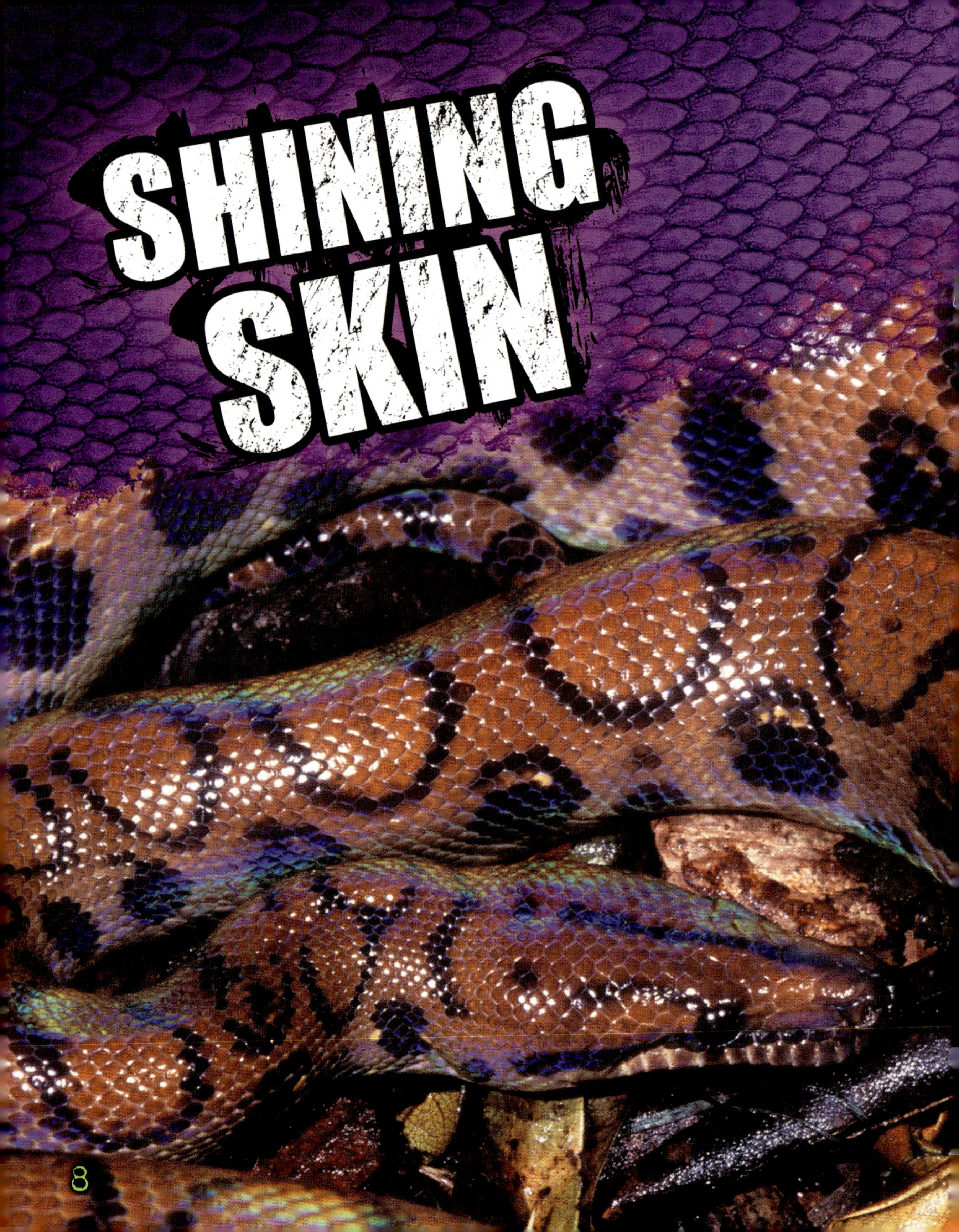

Rainbow boas get their name from their shiny skin. Their **scales** have tiny bumps that **refract** light. This rainbow shine on their scales looks like oil in water.

These snakes usually have red, orange, or brown scales. They have dark circles on their bodies and lines on their heads. These patterns **camouflage** them from **predators**.

Shed Some Layers

A rainbow boa's skin does not grow with its body. That means rainbow boas outgrow and lose their top layer of skin several times a year.

Wild cats and **raptors** are predators that eat rainbow boas. Humans also hunt the snakes for their colorful skins.

CATCHING MEALS

Rainbow boas hunt for **prey** at night. They use **pits** to sense heat from possible meals. Birds, lizards, and **rodents** are their favorites.

Waste No Time

Baby rainbow boas first hunt about a week after birth.

Rainbow Boa Prey

A rainbow boa **strikes** at its dinner. It holds its prey with sharp teeth. Then it **coils** around the animal and **constricts**.

A Tight Squeeze

The rainbow boa squeezes tighter each time the animal breathes out.

The rainbow boa opens wide.
It swallows the animal whole.
Then it slithers off into the night.

On a Diet

Rainbow boas only need to eat about once every ten days.

SPECIES PROFILE

SCIENTIFIC NAME: *EPICRATES CENCHRIA*

NICKNAME: SLENDER BOA

AVERAGE SIZE: 4-7 FEET (1.2-2.1 METERS)

HABITATS: FORESTS, RAIN FORESTS, SAVANNAHS

COUNTRIES: ARGENTINA, BOLIVIA, BRAZIL, COLOMBIA, COSTA RICA, ECUADOR, FRENCH GUIANA, GUYANA, PANAMA, PARAGUAY, PERU, SURINAME, TRINIDAD AND TOBAGO, VENEZUELA

VENOMOUS: NO

HUNTING METHOD: CONSTRICTION

COMMON PREY: RODENTS, BIRDS, LIZARDS, BATS

GLOSSARY

camouflage—to hide an animal by helping it blend in with the surroundings

coils—wraps around

constricts—squeezes until breathing stops

pits—heat-sensing holes around the mouth; rainbow boas use pits to hunt for food at night.

predators—animals that hunt other animals for food

prey—animals that are hunted by other animals for food

rain forests—hot, rainy areas with tall trees

raptors—birds of prey; raptors have excellent vision and sharp talons and beaks.

refract—to shine light back in many colors

rodents—small animals that usually gnaw on their food

savannahs—grassy areas with few trees

scales—small plates of skin that cover and protect a snake's body

scutes—large, rough scales on the stomach of a snake

strikes—bites quickly and with force

TO LEARN MORE

At the Library

Oachs, Emily Rose. *Emerald Tree Boas*. Minneapolis, Minn.: Bellwether Media, 2014.

Raum, Elizabeth. *Boa Constrictors*. Mankato, Minn.: Amicus High Interest, 2014.

Woodward, John. *Everything You Need To Know About Snakes: And Other Scaly Reptiles*. New York, N.Y.: DK Pub., 2013.

On the Web

Learning more about rainbow boas is as easy as 1, 2, 3.

1. Go to www.factsurfer.com.

2. Enter "rainbow boas" into the search box.

3. Click the "Surf" button and you will see a list of related web sites.

With factsurfer.com, finding more information is just a click away.

INDEX

The images in this book are reproduced through the courtesy of: Tiberiu Sahlean, front cover; Trond Larsen, pp. 4-5; Patrick K. Campbell, p. 7; Ardea/ Geoff Trinder/ Animals Animals, pp. 8-9; Minden Pictures/ SuperStock, pp. 10-11; Matt Gibson, p. 12; NHPA/ SuperStock, pp. 13, 17 (bottom), 18-19; Joel Sartore/ Getty Images, pp. 14-15; Erni, p. 15 (top, bottom); Matt Jeppson, p. 15 (middle); Age Fotostock/ Superstock, pp. 16-17; fivespots, pp. 20-21.